W9-BRV-856

Ultimate Cars

PORSCHE

A.T. McKenna

ABDO Publishing Company

visit us at
www.abdopub.com

Published by Abdo Publishing Company, 4940 Viking Drive, Edina, Minnesota 55435.
Copyright © 2000 by Abdo Consulting Group, Inc. International copyrights reserved in all
countries. No part of this book may be reproduced in any form without written permission from
the publisher.

Printed in the United States.

Cover and Interior Photo credits: Corbis, AP/Wideworld, David Gooley

Library of Congress Cataloging-in-Publication Data

McKenna, A. T.
    Porsche / A. T. McKenna.
        p.   cm. -- (Ultimate cars)
    Includes index.
    Summary: Surveys the history of the Porsche and its designs, engines, and performance.
     ISBN 1-57765-124-3
    1. Porsche automobile -- Juvenile literature. [1. Porsche automobile.] I. Title. II. Series.
TL215.P75M38 2000
629.222'1--dc21

                               98-29319
                                 CIP
                                 AC

Contents

Porsche Sports Cars

The Porsche is one of the most exotic sports cars in the world. A sports car is a car that is very fast and has a sporty or race car look to it. It is designed for the fun of driving. Sports cars most often have only two seats.

The Porsche company began in Gmünd, Austria, and has been building cars since 1949. The very first Porsche was built from Volkswagen parts. Some Porsche models include the Boxster, the 911, the 914, and the Spyder.

The Porsche emblem looks similar to the Ferrari logo. In the center is a black horse on a yellow shield. This is the coat of arms for Stuttgart, Germany. Stuttgart was the location of one of the Porsche factories. The background of the emblem has six stag's horns.

The Porsche PanAmericana Showcar looks a little like a dune buggy.

Porches are known for their exceptionally powerful engines. Over the years, these successful race and road cars have competed and won many races, from Le Mans and Monte Carlo, to Can-Am and Paris-Dakar events.

The company found that the more races Porsches won, the more popular its cars became. Everyone wanted a car like the one that had just won in Monte Carlo or Le Mans!

The Porsche name is easily recognized all over the world.

Ferdinand Porsche

Ferdinand Porsche was born in 1875 in the small town of Maffersdorf, Austria. He attended the Imperial Technical School in Reichenberg. Porsche had earned his engineering doctorate from Vienna Technical Institute. He also received an honorary doctorate from the Technical University in Stuttgart.

During this time, electricity was being studied. Soon it was clear that Dr. Porsche was a genius with electricity. He wired his family's home and designed a carriage that could be powered by electricity.

Ferdinand Porsche (left) and his son, Ferry, draw a crowd around one of their early cars on June 10, 1950.

Early cars were powered by batteries. Dr. Porsche built an engine that used gasoline instead of batteries. Combined with electricity, the car was much more efficient. The process of combining gasoline and electricity together is called hybrid power.

On December 1, 1930, Dr. Porsche opened his own engineering and design firm in Stuttgart, Germany. He was 55 years old. His 21-year-old son Ferry joined him. Soon, the business grew so large, that they had to open a bigger factory in Zuffenhausen in 1938.

The people's car, designed by Ferdinand Porsche, under production at a Volkswagen factory in Germany. The first of such factories was opened by Adolf Hitler in 1936.

One of their first projects was a commission by Adolf Hitler to build an affordable car for the German people. This car became the Volkswagen Beetle.

During World War II, Dr. Porsche built tanks and armored weapons for the government. All auto manufacturers were expected to do this. The Porsche factory was damaged during bombing. So, Dr. Porsche moved his engineering, design, and assembly work to Gmünd, Austria.

After the war, Dr. Porsche and his family were imprisoned by the French. Dr. Porsche spent two years in prison in solitary confinement. He was almost 72 years old.

The First Porsche

When Dr. Porsche was released from prison, he moved back to Gmünd. While in prison, he had dreamed about building a car that would be called "Porsche."

The first Porsche car was shown at the Swiss Grand Prix in July, 1948. The body was assembled by hand and made of aluminum. The chassis was a tubular space frame. The chassis is the skeleton of a car. The car was a two-seater called the Type 356-001. It was made of mostly Volkswagen parts. The engine, steering system, and brakes all came from Volkswagen. The car weighed only 1,324 pounds (600 kg).

The 356 reached 85 mph (136 km/h), with a 1.1 liter Volkswagen engine. The V-4 engine produced 40 horsepower at 4,000 rpm. The number after *V* stands for how many cylinders there are in the engine. Most modern cars have four cylinders, V-4. Horsepower is the amount of power the engine has. The initials *rpm* stand for revolutions per minute. This means that while the engine is running, it goes through the same sequence of events thousands of times per minute to keep the fuel flowing through.

The first Porsche was mid-engined. This means the engine was placed in the middle of the car. Later, the engine was placed behind the rear wheels so there was more room inside for passengers. The chassis was made of pressed steel.

Dr. Porsche's son Ferry worked with him to produce the Porsche 356. Only four were produced in 1948, but by 1952, 60 Porsche 356s were released. When Dr. Porsche turned 75 years old in 1950, more than 250 of his sports cars had been sold.

Dr. Porsche died of a stroke on January 30, 1951. His company was on its way to success. Three years after his death, 5,000 356s had been sold.

A Porsche displayed at the 1951 motor show in Earl's Court.

Famous Porsche People

Ferry Porsche shown here on January 24, 1994, died four years later on March 27, 1998.

Ferry Porsche was Dr. Ferdinand Porsche's son. He joined his father in the engineering and design business in 1930 at age 21. Ferry was a talented engineer. He and his father often worked together on projects. Ferry continued running the business after Dr. Porsche's death.

Louise Piech was Ferry's sister. She ran the Porsche factory in Gmünd during the war. By 1946, her successful operation employed 200 workers.

Dr. Anton Piech was Louise's husband. Dr. Piech helped Louise run the factory in Gmünd.

Dr. Piech accepted a job designing a Formula One race car for Piero Dusio, an Italian car maker. The money from this job helped get him and Dr. Porsche out of prison after the war.

Ferdinand Alexander Porsche was Ferry's son. He was called Butzi. He joined the company in 1957 when he was 28 years old. He became the head of the styling department. Butzi designed the Porsche 901 and 904 models.

Louise and Anton's son, Ferdinand Piech, was named the head of engineering in 1965. He focused much of his work on creating Porsche race cars.

Ernst Fuhrmann was a Viennese engineer who designed early Porsche engines. In 1952, he designed a 1.5-liter engine that could go 100 mph (160 km/h). Fuhrmann also designed the Type 547/3 Carrera engine. This engine produced 148 horsepower at 7,500 rpm.

Friedrich Weber worked with Dr. Porsche at Austro-Daimler, another car builder. At the time, Porsche was the chief engineer. Weber was hired to work for Porsche as a craftsman for the Porsche 356.

Ferdinand Piech went on to become the Chairman of Volkswagen. He is shown here posing with the next generation of beetle on January 4, 1999.

Creating a Car

Dr. Porsche knew a lot about building mechanical products. He was a master engineer and had worked on projects for many other car companies. So, he knew what it took to design and build a car when he decided to build his own car.

Building a car takes many people, from designers and engineers to mechanics. First, the designers come up with an idea of how the car should look. The designer usually draws several versions of the car before a design is accepted. Then, the designer makes a clay model of the car.

Designers use wood and foam to make a frame. This frame is the actual size of the car. Then, warm clay is laid over the frame and allowed to cool. This makes a life-sized model of the car. The model is then painted so that it looks like the actual car.

After the model is completed, the engineers work with mechanics to build a prototype. A prototype is a very early version of the car. All the parts on the prototype are tested for strength and quality. The prototype is usually tested on the race track and on the street to see how it handles. The first Porsche was tested on the autobahn and in the Alps.

The prototype is displayed at car shows to see if people like it before the actual cars are produced. If the car is going to be built, changes are made based on the results of the testing and the responses from people who saw it. Usually, when the actual car is complete, it does not look very much like the prototype.

An early Porsche prototype

Here at the Ford plant, cars are produced in large quantities at a fast pace as the car is brought to the workers.

Most cars go through an assembly line when being built. On an assembly line each worker has a specific job to do. The workers line up in rows and perform their jobs as the car moves down the line. One worker may put in the seats, while another installs the wheels.

The Porsche assembly line is not what we think of today, with machinery doing a lot of the work. All Porsches were handbuilt, one at a time.

On an assembly line, each worker has a specific job to perform such as sanding down part of the car before painting.

The Porsche assembly line is actually more of a production line. One car is produced at a time and the engine is assembled separately then placed in the chassis. Today, Porsches are still one of the few cars that are handmade, so the quality is very high. The familiar shape of the Porsche has stayed the same after many years of production.

Porsches are handmade inside the Porsche factory rather than built in mass quantities like other cars.

An assembly line at the Porsche factory

Porsche Timeline

Porsche 356

America Roadsters

Porsche 911

Porsche 914

Porsche Boxster

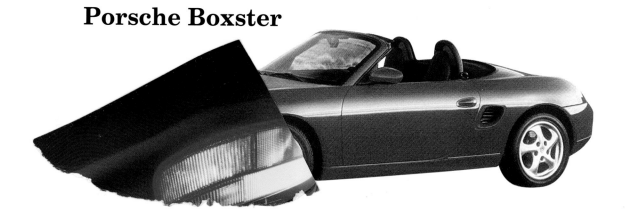

Porsche 911

The Porsche 911 actually started out as the 901. Before production started in 1964, the 901 was changed to the 911. This was because Peugeot, another car manufacturer, had copyrighted all three-number combinations with a zero in the middle. Copyrighting means gaining the legal right to be the only company able to use a name or number for your product.

Butzi Porsche designed the body for this new car. His father wanted a car that would carry two adult passengers and two small children in the back seat. This new car was introduced at the Frankfurt Auto Show in 1963.

It was a classic Porsche, with power, comfort, and more space for people. It was only slightly larger than the Porsche 356. The body was all-steel, which was welded into a single-unit chassis.

The new six-cylinder engine was designed by Ferdinand Piech, and developed by Hans Tomala. This was the first Porsche production car with a V-6 engine. The car could go 124 mph (200 km/h). A production car is a car that is produced for the general public in a larger quantity. It is not a special, limited production car or a race model.

The Porsche 911 Turbo is just a blur on the road.

The engine was placed in the rear of the car. This made the car quite heavy in the back and the front felt like it was floating. The 911 weighed 2,380 pounds (1,079 kg), and 405 of those pounds (184 kg) were the engine and engine accessories. So, the factory offered to install small weights on each side of the front bumper to even out the weight.

Over the years, the 911 body has been modified. In 1967, a new body style called the Targa was developed. This has always been one of the most popular 911 models. The first cars had zip-out back windows like most convertibles had. But because the rear windows were leaky and noisy, Porsche installed glass rear windows in later models. The Porsche 911, which was first produced in 1964, is still going strong today. It is considered the most famous and popular of all Porsche models.

***The sporty Porsche
911 Turbo.***

Porsche 914

Porsche now had a successful sports car with the 911. The Porsche 356 model had been discontinued. Now, Porsche wanted to build an inexpensive car.

At this time, Volkswagen wanted to build a sportier car. Ferry Porsche and Heinz Nordhoff of Volkswagen agreed to work together to build a new car using the Volkswagen 411 engine. It would be called the VW-Porsche in Europe.

Porsche bought some of the bodies and installed its own Porsche engine. These cars would go under the Porsche name in America. Butzi Porsche designed the mid-engine car. It was called the 914.

The 914 was introduced in 1969 at the Frankfurt Auto Show. This car looked distinctly different than the earlier Porsches. But underneath it had all the reliable components of a regular Porsche.

All 914s had a removable roof section and a fixed Targa-type roll bar. The only feature on the outside of the 914 that looked like a Porsche was the lettering behind the roll bar.

Most people did not like the look of the 914. It was thought to be unattractive. And with the success of the previous 911 model, the 914 was a disappointment to many. The 914 was discontinued in 1976.

The Porsche 914

Porsche Boxster

In 1996, Porsche introduced the first new Porsche sports car in 19 years. It was the first mid-engined car since the 914. The Boxster has a 201 horsepower 2.5-liter, water-cooled, six-cylinder engine. The cost of the two-seater Boxster was $39,980 when it first came out. It had an optional hardtop with a heatable rear window that cost $2,249.

An interesting feature of the Boxster is the rear spoiler. A spoiler is like a wing that is mounted to the back or sometimes sides of a sports car. The spoiler on the Boxster raises up in the air when the car reaches 75 mph (121 k/hr). This gives the car a little extra push at higher speeds. When the car goes below 50 mph (80 km/h), the spoiler goes back down.

The first Porsche Boxsters arrived in the United States in January of 1997. More than 10,000 customers had placed advance orders for this all-new sports car.

The Porsche Boxster

Porsche Racing

The first Porsche to compete in auto racing was the 356 model. In 1951, Ferry Porsche raced a Porsche 356 at Le Mans. Le Mans is a famous race that takes place in France. The race lasts 24 hours. Ferry won the race.

In 1953, the Fuhrmann Carrera engine was introduced to use in the Type 550-1500RS racers, the Spyders. This engine was designed by Ernst Fuhrmann. The Spyder was the car to race if you wanted to win. Porsche Spyders were raced all over Europe and the United States in sports car races and Formula One and Formula Two classes.

In 1955, a 356-type race model was produced with a badge that had the word *carrera*, meaning "race" in Spanish, on the rear of the car. By 1961, Porsche had withdrawn from Formula One racing in order to work on other projects.

From 1965 to 1969, Porsches were again the hot racers. Butzi Porsche was named head of engineering in 1965. He became interested in hill climbs, a type of auto racing. Porsches won fourth place at the Daytona 24-hour race and third place at Sebring in 1966. From 1967 to 1970, Porsche 911s won countless races and world endurance records.

In 1980, Porsche ran a car in the Indianapolis 500. The car didn't do well. In 1988, Porsche decided to try again. This time driver Teo Fabi took ninth place. By 1990, Porsche decided to get out of Indy car racing due to changes in the rules.

Porsche has had a long history in auto racing. Today, Porsche cars are raced in sports car races and vintage races all over Europe. The cars are known for being fast and competitive.

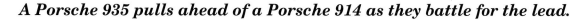

A Porsche 935 pulls ahead of a Porsche 914 as they battle for the lead.

Porsche in America

Porsches were popular in Europe and cost about half the price of a Ferrari. But the cars were not well known in the United States until 1952.

Max Hoffman, an automotive distributor who brought Jaguar, Mercedes-Benz, and other foreign cars to the United States, wanted to bring Porsches to America as well.

Porsche produced 16 aluminum-bodied America Roadsters in 1952 for Hoffman to import. These cars were made for racing on America's race tracks. They were lightweight and fast. The cars cost $4,600. These Porsche cars became well-known in the United States. So, Porsche designed a car for everyday driving in America. It was called the

The modern Porsche Speedster.

Speedster. At $2,995, these convertible cars sold like crazy.

From 1955 to 1959, Porsche sold more than 3,600 Speedsters in America. With the hardtop removed and the windshield detached, the Speedster looked like an overturned bathtub.

A mid 1950's bathtub Porsche.

Today, Porsche is still importing cars to the United States with great success. The latest model to reach the United States is the Porsche 911 Carrera. The 1999 model was priced at $65,000, much more than the early models. Top speed for the 911 Carrera is 174 mph (280 km/h) at 7,300 rpm.

The popular Porsche 911 Cabriolet.

Glossary

autobahn- a German, Swiss, or Austrian highway. Drivers can travel on the autobahn at very high speeds.

commission - an assignment given to a person or company to build or make something.

convertible - a car with a top that can be removed. Convertibles can have soft tops or hard tops.

coupe - a car with a permanent top.

doctorate - the degree earned by a doctor of philosophy. Also called a PhD.

Formula One - a kind of race in which people drive single-seat cars. The insides of the cars have no luxuries, only the basic instruments required for driving.

hybrid - something made of two different separate elements.

Internet Sites

**Porsche
http://www.usporsche.com/isapi/english/start/
default.asp**

This is Porsche's official site. Read about the history of the company, learn about clubs and events, and take an online factory tour. Click on the 911 or the Boxster to learn about new models.

**The Sports Car Club of America
http://www.scca.org**

This is the official site of the Sports Car Club of America. Learn about the SCCA, scheduled racing events, and accredited racing schools. Get information on SCCA pro racing, and a road rally that everyone can compete in.

These sites are subject to change. Go to your favorite search engine and type in "Porsche" for more sites.

Index